Blooming Lovely

A Collection of Cold Porcelain Fl

Just A Lovely Bunch of Flowers!

FIRST EDITION - October 2014

Published by A M Reynolds Publishing
The Yews, Lein Road, Kingston on Spey
Fochabers, Moray IV32 7NW

ISBN No. 978-0-9571554-2-8

A catalogue record for this book is available from the British Library.

Written by Alyson Reynolds
Design and Layout, Photography and Drawings by Alyson Reynolds © 2014
Printed and Bound by MMS Almac Ltd, Keith, AB55 5DD

 The FSC (Forest Stewardship Council) logo certifies that the paper used in this book originated from forests that are managed in a sustainable way.

All flowers and arrangements contained within this book have been made by the author

Contents

Introduction

Blooming Lovely! *is a compilation of the Teaching Collection Cards that I produced following requests from students on how to make some of those popular flowers not included in my first two books.*

The Collection covers flowers from all seasons and includes suggestions for others that can be made with similar techniques and structure. All the flowers in the photographs are made from Cold Porcelain. With Christmas tending to be 'just around the corner' I have included some Festive Seasonal favourites together with a few ideas for decorations to impress your guests. I've even had the chance to correct some of those classic spelling mistakes!

As with 'Autumn Glory' and 'Down the Garden Path', I encourage you to explore your own creativity and colour schemes. There are no boundaries and you have nothing to lose, only something more to gain!

Enjoy ...

Alysan

Equipment and Techniques

Cold Porcelain

Cold porcelain is an air drying paste made from PVA glue, cornflower and baby oil - simple. All you need is a little muscle power to keep stirring when you are making it. Recipe Below.

Cold porcelain dries hard but is not brittle. If you roll the paste very fine, when dry there may be some flex which can add softness to the petals in the overall flower. Cold porcelain can shrink when dry. The recipe below has approx 5% shrinkage - some commercial pastes can shrink 15-20%. You will need to add white Acrylic paint before use to prevent the paste drying opaque.

If you keep the cold porcelain wrapped in cling film and in an air tight container it will last. I find it better to make a small amount at a time - about 250 - 300 gms. You can use it straight away. Information regarding colouring is on page 8.

Ingredients • 1 cup of a good PVA glue • 1 cup good quality cornflour • 1 - 2 Tablespoons baby oil

Put the oil and glue in a NON-STICK saucepan and mix together with a wooden spoon. Stir in the cup of cornflour and mix it well in. Place over a low heat stirring constantly until like choux pastry it gathers around the spoon. It will get lumpy at first but keep going. When it rolls into a ball without sticking to your hands it's ready. Take off the heat and gently knead to clear any big lumps. Let it cool a little then rap in cling film and keep in an airtight container. You can use it straight away.

Tools

The photograph below shows all the tools and materials I have used to create the flowers within this book. The same tools, cutters and veiner that are used with Sugarcraft can be used with cold porcelain. It is surprising how many different effects can be achieved by using these tools in different ways. It is not always easy to explain in writing how to use the tools however. Perseverance is the key and coupled with practice comes knowledge.

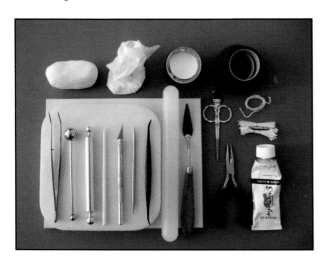

1. Cold Porcelain
2. Corn flour
3. PVA Glue
4. Florists Tapes
5. Cel Board
6. Cel Pad
7. Surgical Tweezers
8. Ball Tool large
9. Ball Tool
10. Ceramic Veining Stick
11. Scalpel
12. Smooth cel stick
13 Jem Dresden/Veining tool
14. Rolling Pin
15. Palette Knife
16. Scissors
17. Pliers
18. Stamens
19. Embroidery Thread
20. White Acrylic Paint

Tools

The most useful tools for me are the ball tool, the ceramic silk veining tool, a pair of sharp nail scissors and surgical tweezers.

Use the ball tool to create softly curled petals and also to cup them.

For a gentle curl along the edge of a petal, place the ball half on and half off the edge of the paste and gently push forward with a smooth continuous motion around the whole shape. A gentle cupped effect is achieved by placing the ball tool just inside but away from the edge of the petal, and work as above. For deeply cupped petals, place the ball tool in the centre of the petal and make small circular motions which will curl up the sides.

Use the ceramic cel stick to create varied textured finishes on the paste by rolling the tip or whole stick one way or back and forth. The tip can make an excellent ragged edge.

Cutters

I use both metal and plastic cutters however when working with cold porcelain I find metal cutters give a sharper cut. I have used KIT BOX, FMM and Tinker Tech cutters, plus hand drawn templates throughout this book. If paste is sticking to the cutter, rub a little cold cream around the edge before use, OR lightly dust cornflour onto the paste before cutting out. Keep your cutters clean - they will cut better and last longer.

KB - Kit Box Cutters
TT - Tinker Tech Cutters
FMM - FMM Sugarcraft Cutters

Petal and Leaf Veiner

Cold Porcelain works well with both ceramic and rubber veiner. I have used mainly Squires Kitchen Great Impressions double sided veiner as they have an excellent range. Dust a little cornflour onto a ceramic veiner before use to avoid the paste sticking.

Wash veiner with warm soapy water before use to avoid transferring specs of colour onto clean paste. Red spots are my nemesis in this respect.

Florist tape

Gently pull the florist tape to release the gum whilst wrapping tightly down and around the stem. I have suggested widths of tape to use throughout, however use what you are comfortable with. The less tape for individual petals the better.

Wires

In general cut your wires longer rather than shorter as it is easier to cut them off than it is to add them on. I use white wires for petals and green for leaves. The lower the gauge number the thicker the wire.

Varnishing

To achieve a very high gloss shine, use full strength confectioner's varnish. Remove and spin the stem between your fingers and thumb to get rid of excess varnish.

For a softer shine mix equal quantities of confectioner's varnish with isopropanol alcohol (available from chemists) to get ½ strength varnish. You can also mix these two in ¼ and ¾ ratios (alcohol to varnish) to get varied 'shine' results., PME Edible Glaze - comes in a spray can, easy to use and gives a gloss finish.

Super Matt Sealing Spray from The Cromartie Group - comes in both gloss or matt finish. Hairspray is a good alternative as it also seals in the colour.

When using spray cans to varnish or for long periods of dusting with coloured powders, work in a ventilated area and wear a mask to avoid inhalation

Making leaves

Many leaves look similar in both shape, colour and veining. If you don't have a cutter and veiner for a particular flower, use leaf shapes such as rose, hydrangea and grapevine to give variety. It is amazing how you can change a leaf by colour and finish. Gloss and matt varnishing works wonders. In this book the main focus is on the flower and the foliage although important is not always critical in an arrangement - unless, of course, it is an exhibition piece!

Don't be afraid to take a leaf from the garden, cover with a little Vaseline, place it over the paste and roll over the top to get the true vein impression.

C LOURING

For each flowers subject I have photographed and named some colours which I have used for the flowers. These are only to give you a guide. There are many shades of colour by different manufacturers and I have hardly ever used a single one on it's own. A good selection of brushes helps considerably and be bold in mixing your colours to get the result you want.

Base Colours

Always add white acrylic paint to your porcelain before using. This prevents the porcelain appearing opaque when dry. Add base colour to your porcelain AFTER the white acrylic has been added. I have used the following paste colours within this book - Spruce Green (mid to dark green), Gooseberry (lime green) Dusky Pink, Grape Violet (purple), Cream, Tangerine and Melon (yellow).

Using colour dusts

1. Dust with colour when the cold porcelain is damp this way the colour will be absorbed into the paste as it dries.
2. Put a little dust onto a kitchen paper towel, dip in brush and tap off the excess to avoid applying too much at once.
3. In general dust from the bottom upwards to give a smooth even finish. Keep a couple of brushes to use to mix colours.
4. Experiment with colours. If you put darker colours on first, it will not be easy to lift the shade by adding lighter colours on top. Start with a lighter colour and you will have more control by adding depth and shading.
5. To make a paint, mix colour dust with a little water or clear alcohol (gin/vodka). Be careful not to make it too runny.
6. To make your own pollen, put some fine semolina into a small clear pot with a lid. Add in some colour dust and shake well. The depth of colour is controlled by the amount of colour dust used.
7. A selection of brushes of different widths and shapes is useful including very fine ones for painting.

Effects on leaves and petals

To reflect a 'crinkled edge' on your leaf, use a cel stick to roll firmly around the edge. Highlight the 'crinkle' with another colour, either lighter or darker than the main leaf.

To create a leaf to look like it has been nibbled or split, make a small cut through the front with a scalpel. Open it up slightly and dust around the edges of the split using a mix of dark green and aubergine.

Making a small tear along the edge of the leaf at an angle can be equally as effective and using different colours to highlight the tear gives another wonderful view of nature in it's true form.

WINTER INTO SPRING

As the Snowdrops pop up through the tough winter ground signalling the promise of Spring approaching, these hardy little flowers are well aware that it is quite likely that another frost may come and try to test their courage!

In the vein of thought that 'less is more', the Snowdrop is a perfect example. With pure white flowers, touched with the brightest green on the tips of their petals attached to the end of slender stems and nestling in amongst a backdrop of tall straight leaves, these pretty flowers can make a beautiful display in the simplest way.

With the same approach, another pretty flower to raise the Spirit is the Primrose or Primula. There are many varieties in colour and form that you can be sure to find one to match any theme.

Left: Stems of Cold Porcelain Snowdrops and leaves, wired into a bunch and inserted into some dry oasis, placed in a small terracotta flower-potand covered with some natural moss off the roof of the garden shed!

Right: Cold Porcelain Primrose flowers stemsand leaves, individually placed into dry oasis, again using a delightful mini watering can which I found in the flower section inAsda for £3.50 (and that included the real Busy Lizzie!)

SNOWDROPS

It is always encouraging to see the snowdrops as they start to pop up through the snow - almost defying the odds!

For such delicate flowers they are remarkably hardy. With their pure white petals contrasting sharply with shades of green lanky foliage they appear precise in their appearance, but actually come in many shapes and sizes.

Bringing an inkling of new beginnings to a rather drab garden, they are left well alone to spread their cheer from late January to March, when the comes out and trims them back to earth!

Equipment
Ball Tool, scalpel, small sharp scissors, cel stick, jem tool
Snowdrop petal cutters TT or template
Narrow leaf cutters KB - or template

Materials
White and pale green Cold Porcelain or Flower Paste
26 & 24g green wire
White thread
Nile or dark green florist tape
Colours: Gooseberry green paste,
Dusts: spring, medium & dark green, yellow,
White acrylic paint if using cold porcelain

Snowdrop Centres

1. Tape 3 strands of white thread approximately 1cm long onto the end of a 26g green wire with 1/2 width Nile green florist tape.

2. Roll a small ball of pale green paste and insert the wire through the ball up to just covering the base of the threads, pulling it into a small teardrop shape.

3. Trim the thread to be about 5mm in length and paint the ends with yellow dust mixed with water.

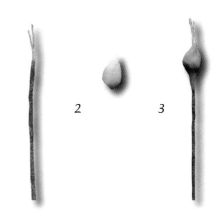

Inside Petal

4. Roll out some fine white paste. Using the smaller cutter, cut out a petal.

5. Soften the edges with a ball tool, but be careful not to lose the shape.

6. Score down the outside of the petal with a jem tool or cocktail stick.

7. Dab a little glue on the base of the centre and thread the stem through the petal so that the scored side is showing on the outside and secure.

8. Mix some light green dust with water and paint a rim of green around the bottom of each petal. Paint some light green straight lines down the inside of each petal as shown.

Make a few of these and leave to dry off a little before adding outer petals.

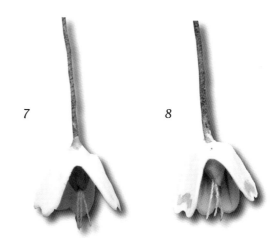

Outer Petals

9. Roll out some fine white paste and cut out a petal using the larger pointed cutter,

10. Soften the edges with a ball tool as before. Score down the outside of the petal with a jem tool or cocktail stick and cup the individual petals.

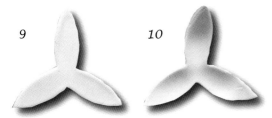

11. Dab a little glue on the base of first petal and thread the stem through the outer petal so that the scored side is showing on the outside. Press down gently and secure.

12. Roll a small hip of green paste and thread the bud through the centre and secure with a little glue to the neck of the flower.

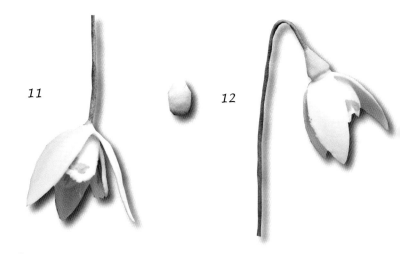

11   *12*

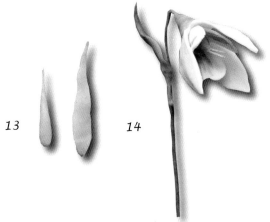

13   *14*

Calyx

13. Roll a slim cone of green paste approx 2cm in length and squash flat between finger and thumb to make a single calyx.

14. Bend the neck of the snowdrop just below the base of the hip and attach the calyx with glue directly onto the wire a little below it. Curl the side of the calyx in towards eachother and give it a little twist. Dust the hip and the calyx with shades of green.

Closed Buds

15. Roll a slim oval approx 1.5 cm in length. Glue and insert a hooked 26g wire in one end and secure. Score down the outside of the bud with a jem tool or cocktail stick.

Follow steps 12 to 14 to finish. These are quick and effective so make several and vary the sizes of your buds for interest.

15

Opening Buds

16. Follow step 15 as for closed buds and then steps 9 to 16.

At step 11 pull down the petals close to the bud leaving them just a little open at the bottom.

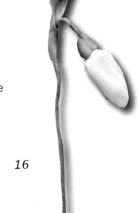

16

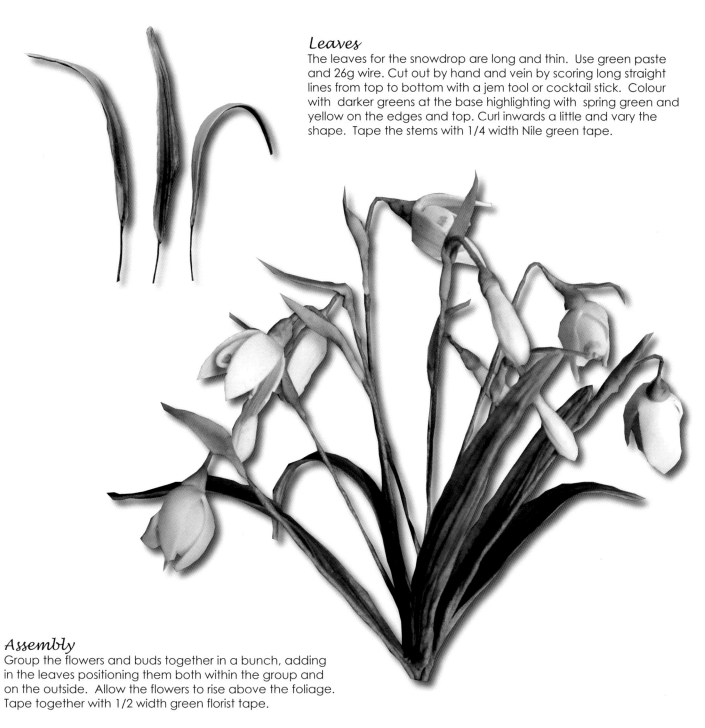

Leaves

The leaves for the snowdrop are long and thin. Use green paste and 26g wire. Cut out by hand and vein by scoring long straight lines from top to bottom with a jem tool or cocktail stick. Colour with darker greens at the base highlighting with spring green and yellow on the edges and top. Curl inwards a little and vary the shape. Tape the stems with 1/4 width Nile green tape.

Assembly

Group the flowers and buds together in a bunch, adding in the leaves positioning them both within the group and on the outside. Allow the flowers to rise above the foliage. Tape together with 1/2 width green florist tape.

13

Templates

Cold Porcelain Snowdrops

Snowdrop petals
Small - full size hand drawn based on TT shape

Snowdrop petals
Large - full size hand drawn based on TT shape

Snowdrop leaves
hand drawn - freestyle!

Colouring

Use spring green for painting onto the petals. For the leaves use a good mix of mid and dark green with spring and yellow to highlight. You can brush the petals with white, or Bridal Satin to give a little shimmer if you wish.

White, Primrose,   Spring, Leaf, Moss and Forrest Green

PRIMROSES

What would we do without these cheerful little flowers in their abundance of colour - some surviving all through the year! Whether Primroses or Primulas it really doesn't matter they make a lovely display in their various colours, shapes and sizes.

Some have petals which are smooth and clearly defined, whilst others are more ragged around the edges. (Not to dissimilar to the difference between me and a super model!) However, beauty is in the eye of the beholder and these are another little treasure to add to the collection.

Equipment
Ball Tool, scalpel, small sharp scissors,
Textured veining stick, star cone tool
Primrose cutter FMM or template
Primrose leaf cutter or template
Primrose leaf veiner SKGI - optional
Calyx cutter or template

Materials
Yellow and green Cold Porcelain or Flower paste
Ball tool
26, 24g green wire
Nile green florist tape
Colours: green & yellow paste,
Dusts: spring, medium & dark green, yellow,
White acrylic paint if using cold porcelain

Flower

1. Roll a cone of yellow paste approx 2cm tall. Flatten the base by pressing it on a firm surface.

2. Using your first fingers and thumbs, gently tease out the bottom half of the cone, thinning the paste between your fingers into a skirt.

3. Place the Primrose cutter over the top of the flattened cone and cut out.

4. Using your ball tool, soften around the petals, spreading them slightly but be careful not to lose the shape.

5. Use a star tool to make an indentation into the centre of the face of the flower. Swap to a textured veining tool and softly roll along the petals, spreading the paste and frilling the edges.

6. Dab a little glue onto the tip of a small stamen, and dip into yellow pollen. Insert into the centre of the flower.

7. Hook a 4" length of 26g green wire, glue and insert into the base of the flower approx 1cm. Tape the stem with 1/2 width green florist tape.

8. Dust the inside of the centre impression with a spring green colour dust. Be careful not to spread it too far outside the centre. Mix a little deep yellow colour dust with water and with a fine brush paint around the outside of the green centre leaving a 2mm space between the green and the yellow.

I tend to make all my flowers in a very pale yellow which allows me to paint or dust them in different colours at this stage. See the final spray at the back

9. Roll out some thin green paste and cut out a calyx.

10. Insert the flower stem down through the calyx. When you reach the base of the flower, put a little glue onto each sepal of the calyx and secure by pressing gently onto the flower. Dust the calyx with mid green.

9

10

11   *12*   *13*

Buds

11. Roll a slim oval of yellow paste approx 1.5cm in length. Shape into a bud. Glue and insert a hooked 26g wire in one end and secure. Tape with 1/2 width green tape.

12. Using fine scissors or a scalpel, gently score or cut half way down the outside of the top of the bud.

13. Cut out a calyx and add to the bud as described at points 9 &10 above. Vary the sizes of your buds for interest.

Leaves

14. Roll out some green paste, leaving it slightly thicker at one end. Place the leaf cutter over the paste with the bottom at the thick end. Cut out your leaf and insert a 26g green wire into the centre of the thick end. Using your ball tool elongate and soften the edges of the leaf, blending any thick paste in. Tape stems with 1/2 width green tape.

15. Place the leaf onto the veiner and press gently.
(If veining by hand, sometimes the veins on our own hands make good impressions with a little help from a jem tool to highlight stronger central veins.)

14   *15*

16

16. Use a mix of colour dusts with different shades of greens together with a touch of yellow and brown to bring your leaves to life.

Make several different sizes cutting them out by hand following the template shape.

Assembly

Tape a group of flowers together into a stem adding a few leaves at the base. I have made some like this and popped them into a small flowerpot with garden soil - look just like the real thing!

Templates

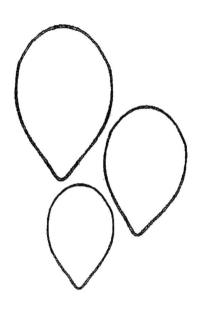

Calyx
KB A002

Cold Porcelain Primroses

Hand drawn
Primrose Petals

Primrose leaf template

Colouring

If you don't have a flower infront of you to copy, Google some images and you will be amazed at the variety around. Brush colour dusts and paint from the inside out to the edge of the petal.

Primrose, Orange, Red, Purple, Spring Green, Leaf Green, Moss Green and Brown

SPRING TO SUMMER

With so much choice you could go on forever! The following popular garden flowers are brought to life with new techniques that again can be adapted and used for creating different flowers.

From the alternative ways of creating stamens to the simplicity of increasing or reducing sizes of petals, the opportunities are endless to explore.

On pages 54 and 55 I have given suggestions of how to try out these techniques to make other flowers to add to your repertoire ; and together these will complement the flowers you will find in Autumn Glory and Down the Garden Path.

Left: Cold Porcelain Foxgloves, Wild Roses, Alstromeria, Thistles and Heather.

CLEMATIS MONTANA

This fabulous climber is the most prolific rambling plant in my garden - but one of the most welcome. Very hardy it wakes up in March with light green, changing to dark green and aubergine foliage. This is followed by an explosion of pink and white flowers from April to late August. Left untamed it will cover everything in its path, climb trees and run underground to spring up somewhere else. Excellent to take cuttings from. Very beautiful indeed and if you want to hide something, grow one of these!

Equipment
Ball tool, scalpel, scissors
Rose petal cutters KB 0052
Clematis Montana petal veiner SKGI
Clematis Montana leaf cutters TT
Peony leaf veiner SKGI

Materials
White acrylic paint - cold porcelain
White and pale green paste
28, 26, 20g green wire
Burgundy florist tape
Pale yellow thread
Seed head stamens - medium
Colours: Gooseberry green paste,
Dusts: shades of pinks, purples, greens,
yellow and brown

Centres

1. Wrap pale yellow thread around 2 fingers about 60 times. Take off your fingers and twist into a figure of eight.

2. Hook over a 28g wire and twist tightly to secure.

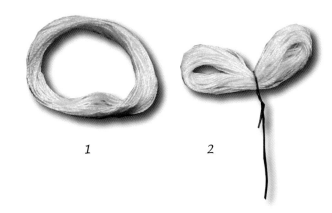

1   2

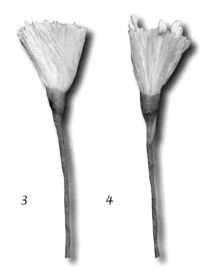

3   4

3. Fold the two sides of thread up and with Nile green florist tape, tape over the hook and down the stem. Cut through the threads and even off the top.

4. Take six medium sized seed head stamens and dust with cream. Lightly colour the centre threads with spring green and tape the stamens around the centre so they are sticking up above the top of the threads.

Buds

5. Roll some cones of white paste of varied sizes from 1cm - 2cm. Glue and insert a hooked 28g wire. Tape the stem with 1/4 width burgundy florist tape.

6. Using the back of a scalpel press some indents around the buds.

7. Dust the base with soft spring green and colours the top with pink or plum. Highlight the indents with darker pink.

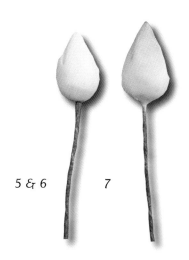

5 & 6   7

Petals

8. Cut out 4 petals from white paste. Glue and insert a 28g wire.

9. Use the ball tool to soften the edges and stretch the paste up into shape. Vein with the SKGI Clematis Montana veiner.

10. Colour the petals with a mix of plum and burgundy shimmer by dusting lightly with a soft brush from the bottom upwards leaving lighter shades in the middle working darker toward the outside. Tape all stems with 1/4 width burgundy florist tape.

8   9   10

11

11. Tape the petals one by one tightly to the base of the flower centre. Each petal has it's own space so position them individually to get a really free flowing flower!

12. From green paste cut out a selection of leaves. Use a 28g wire for the smaller ones and 26g for the larger ones. Soften and vein using the Peony veiner.

The colours are fresh green in the early stages but quickly turn to a much deeper green with a rich burgundy colour of the stems. Use aubergine and browns to achieve this colour.

Tape the stems with burgundy florist tape and join the leaves together in two's and three's - small and large together - any combination seems to work on my climber!

12

Assembly

I love putting this flower together as it really doesn't seem to matter how you do it! It is a full and trailing plant so unless I need it for it's length I usually keep it to smaller sprigs of 3 flowers and a mix of buds.

Using burgundy tape, start with a leading bud or flower by taping it onto a 20g wire. Tape together a couple of buds with some leaves and add this stem onto the main shoot. Continue down the stem adding in flowers, buds and leaves just where you feel they fit to the shape you want. Add in stronger wires if it needs support.

Templates

Cold Porcelain Clematis Montana

FT Clematis Montana Leaves

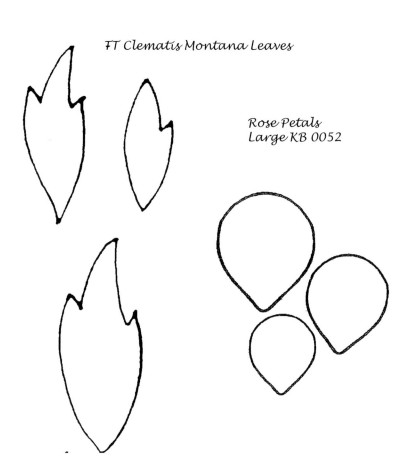

*Rose Petals
Large KB 0052*

Colouring

This Clematis Montana has soft colouring, but the strength of colour in each flower varies. Be adventurous with pale and more vivid flowers.

Burgundy Shimmer, Pink, Cream, Plum, Spring Green, Leaf Green, Daffodil, Aubergine

ALSTROMERIA - 'Princess Diana'

I acquired this Alstromeria from a 'sale' table at the local garden centre. Looking very sad with only a sticky label and a name I took pity, bought it for £2.50 and stuck it in the garden. It wasn't until it came into bloom that I realised how beautiful and different it was in colouring to others I had previously known. Very pleased with myself for finding such a bargain.

In full bloom the yellows and reds are rich and strong, but fade as time goes by to soft, melancholy hues of a fading sunset.

Materials

Pale Yellow and green cold porcelain or flower paste
26 and 20g green wire
Green and white florist tape
Brown pollen
Colours: Gooseberry green, Melon paste,
Dusts: shades of yellow, green, soft red/burgundy and brown
Very fine paint brush
White acrylic paint for cold porcelain

Equipment

Ball tool, scalpel, jem tool, scissors
Alstromeria petal & leaf cutter set KB 0101
Alstromeria petal veiner SKGI
Calyx cutter - medium or template

Centre Stamens

1. Twist/spin a long piece of 1/4 width white florist tape, stretching gently as you go. Cut 6 lengths of 4cm each. Tape them to a 4" length of 26g wire with 1/2 width green tape. Dust over the stamens with a soft burgundy/red.

2. Snip the tips of the stamens into different lengths. Dip the tips into your glue and then into brown pollen. (This pollen can be made by mixing semolina with brown colour dust.) Leave to dry.

1   *2*

Inside petal

3, From pale yellow paste, cut out 3 petals, glue and insert a 4" length of 26g wire. Soften the edges with a ball tool and vein. Tape stems with 1/4 width green tape.

4. Dust the front of the petal with yellow starting from the bottom and becoming little paler at the tip. Do the same for the back of the petal but make it slightly paler overall.

5. Using burgundy/red, dust the tip of the front petal as shown. Use dark brown or aubergine dust mixed with water to paint a central line down the front and mark small dashes on either side.

6. For the back of the petal dust the tip softly with burgundy/red as shown. Shape the petal bending backwards and leave to dry in a cardboard fruit tray which acts perfectly as a former.

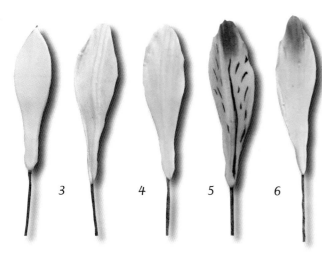

3   *4*   *5*   *6*

Outside petal

7. Using pale yellow paste cut out 3 petals, glue and insert a 4" length of 26g wire. Soften the edges, vein and tape stems with 1/4 width green tape.

8. Again, dust the front of the petal with yellow leaving it paler in the centre. Dust through the centre with burgundy/red, darker in the middle, softening towards the edges. Dust over the tip with mid green and paint a short line down the centre of the petal as shown with brown or burgundy dust mixed with water.

9. For the back, dust yellow and run your burgundy/red brush lightly down the centre. This is not as dark in colour. Brush the tip and the bottom of the petal lightly with green. Shape and dry as for the inside petal.

7   *8*   *9*

Attaching petals

10. Using 1/4 width florist tape, secure the inner petals evenly around the base of the stamens.

11. Use 1/4 width tape to add on the outer petals positioning them in between the first set, keeping them as neat as possible around the base. Try not to make the base become too bulky.

10

11

Calyx

12. From green paste make a cone, flatten out the bottom and cut out a calyx. Soften around the edges with your ball tool.

13. Use your cell stick to make a hole in the centre of calyx. Insert the flower, down through the opened centre. Dab a little glue onto each sepal and secure onto the flower petals. Pinch of any excess paste from the cone of the calyx. Dust with mid to light green.

13

Buds

14. Using the same technique as point 12, cut out a calyx. Using your ball tool soften the edges but stretch the sepals so they are longer.

15. Make a hole in the centre with a cel stick and using the back of your scalpel press a crease into the centre of each sepal.

16. Glue and insert a 26g green wire into the bottom of the calyx. Place a little glue onto each sepal and pinch them together at the top as shown. Try to keep a bud shape and not squash it flat. Dust with mid and light greens and tape the stem with 1/4 width green tape.

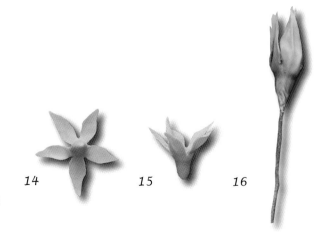

14   15   16

29

Leaves

Use green paste and the template or cutters to make a selection of leaves in various sizes. Hand vein using the jem tool by scoring a central vein and run off smaller veins from the base of the leaf outwards like a fan. I made my own veiner for these by taking a leaf from the garden and using a silicone kit.

Assembly

These flowers grow together in groups on a main stem. With green florist tape, attach a flower to the top a 20g wire. Add on more flowers and buds securing to the main stem and add in a few leaves at the base of where you join flower and stem.

Make a few stems, add some extra leaves and suddenly you have a whole plant. Try different colouring - there are so many varieties to choose from.

Templates

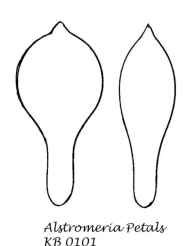

Alstromeria Petals
KB 0101

Calyx

Alstromeria Leaves,
hand drawn from plant

Cold Porcelain Alstromeria

Colouring

Be adventurous with your colouring. Use the colour shades below to make the 'Princess Diana' Alstromeria, but experiment with pinks, oranges, reds - there are so many variations to choose from. If you don't have a garden centre nearby, just Google Alstromeria images and take your pick!

Primrose, Daffodil, Burgundy, Red, Spring Green, Leaf Green, Forrest Green and Brown

FOXGLOVE

In shades of pinks, purples and white the tall, majestic and stately Foxgloves tower above their fellow plants in the flowerbed at the front of The Yews. Rising 6 - 8ft in height they provide a welcoming treat for the bumble bees and a very pretty picture offering an abundance of independent flowers throughout June, July and August.

Self seeding they spread like wildfire and are a real 'must have' cottage garden plant!

Equipment
Ball tool, scalpel, scissors, cel stick
Foxglove cutters KB 0214
Foxglove leaf veiner SKGI
Small to medium calyx cutters KB A002
Multi purpose metal leaf cutters KB A09
Fine Paint brush

Materials
White acrylic paint for cold porcelain
White, pale green and cream paste
30, 28, 26, 20g green wire
Nile green & white florist tape
Yellow pollen
Colours: Gooseberry green liquid paste,
Dusts: pinks, purples, greens, yellow, rust
and brown

Stamens

1. Spin and twist 1/4 width tape tightly between your fingers. Cut 4 x 6cm lengths.

2. Dip one end into yellow pollen and tape onto a 28g green wire at varying heights.

3. Roll a small ball of white paste, insert the stem down through the ball and secure over the join of the tape to the wire.

1　　*2*　　*3*

Flowers

4. Roll some white paste approx 1.5mm thick and cut out a petal.

4　　*5*

5. Soften the edges with a ball tool, spread and stretch out the paste increasing the size to make bigger flowers if needed.

6. Lightly dust both sides of the petal in your chosen colour - slightly softer on the inside and lay the stamen onto the petal.

7. Lightly glue down one side and roll around your finger and secure. Use a ball tool or cel stick to help smooth out the join. (I admit I find this quite fiddly!)

7

6

8. With a very fine brush, paint in some small circles and dots using a deeper shade of colour of the main flower.

9. Using pale green paste, cut out a flat calyx and detach one sepal. Soften and spread the remaining sepals.

10. Insert the flower down through the calyx and secure. Dust with soft green and dot with brown paint. You can do this before or after attaching it to the flower.

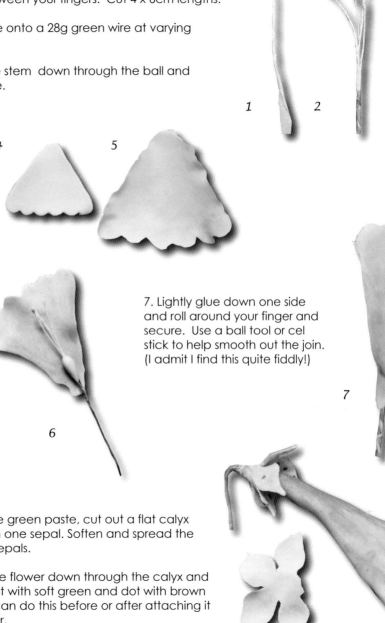

8　　　　　　　　　　　　*9*　　　*10*

33

Buds

11. Roll an oval of pale green paste. Using a scalpel indent a line like a smile over the top. Dust with pale greens and pink/purple on the top.

12. Cut out a green calyx, detach a sepal, soften the edges and secure to the bud. These seem to be slightly thinner on the buds, Dust with greens.

Seed Pods

13. Twist a piece of 1/4 width white tape approx 6 cm in length and tape to a 28g wire. Dust the top 1cm with rust.

14. Roll a 1.5cm pale green cone and insert the wire down through the top to cover the join of the tape and wire. Dust with soft green and a touch of rust.

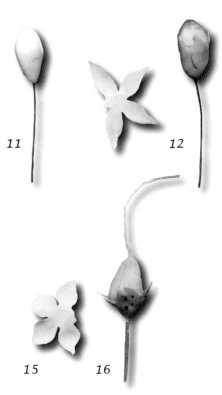

11   *12*

15. Cut out a small calyx, detach one sepal and soften with the ball tool, rounding the remaining sepals. Dust with soft greens.

16. Insert the seed pod down through the calyx and secure. With a fine brush dot the calyx with brown paint.

14

15   *16*

Stem Leaves

17. Roll a thin cone of pale green paste about 1.5 - 2 cm max. Insert as 30g wire and squash flat between your fingers keeping the shape with a point at the top end.

18. Dust with shades of green. These leaves fit tightly to the stem in between the flowers and buds. Tape 1cm down the stem with Nile green tape.

19. From green paste, cut out a selection of leaves in different sizes from pale green paste. Soften the edges, round off the top and vein.

20. Dust with shades of soft greens and run your brush up the centre vein with some plum to highlight. Tape stems 2cm with Nile green tape.

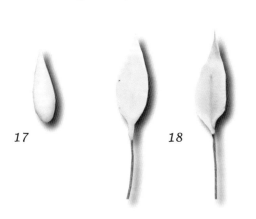

17   *18*

19   *20*

Top buds

21, Roll a very small cone of pale green paste. Insert a 28g wire. Roll several more small cones and secure them to eachother around the initial cone with a little glue. Dust with soft greens and brush the tips with a little plum.

Assembly

Using 1/2 width Nile green tape, secure the top buds on their stem onto a 24g wire. Add in a couple of small leaves and the buds, building in size on their way down the stem. Add in the flowers , again building in size, giving each flower room to move freely. Tape the seed buds onto the stem below the flowers and intersperse with some of the larger leaves.

Templates

Multi-purpose Leaf
KB A09

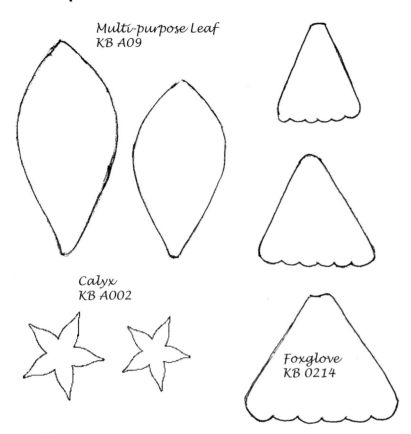

Calyx
KB A002

Foxglove
KB 0214

Cold Porcelain Foxgloves

Colouring

The Foxglove comes in colours of white to pinks and purples and many have varied patterns and colours on the inside.

Lavender, Pink, Plum, Violet, Spring Green, Leaf Green, Daffodil and Brown

WILD ROSES

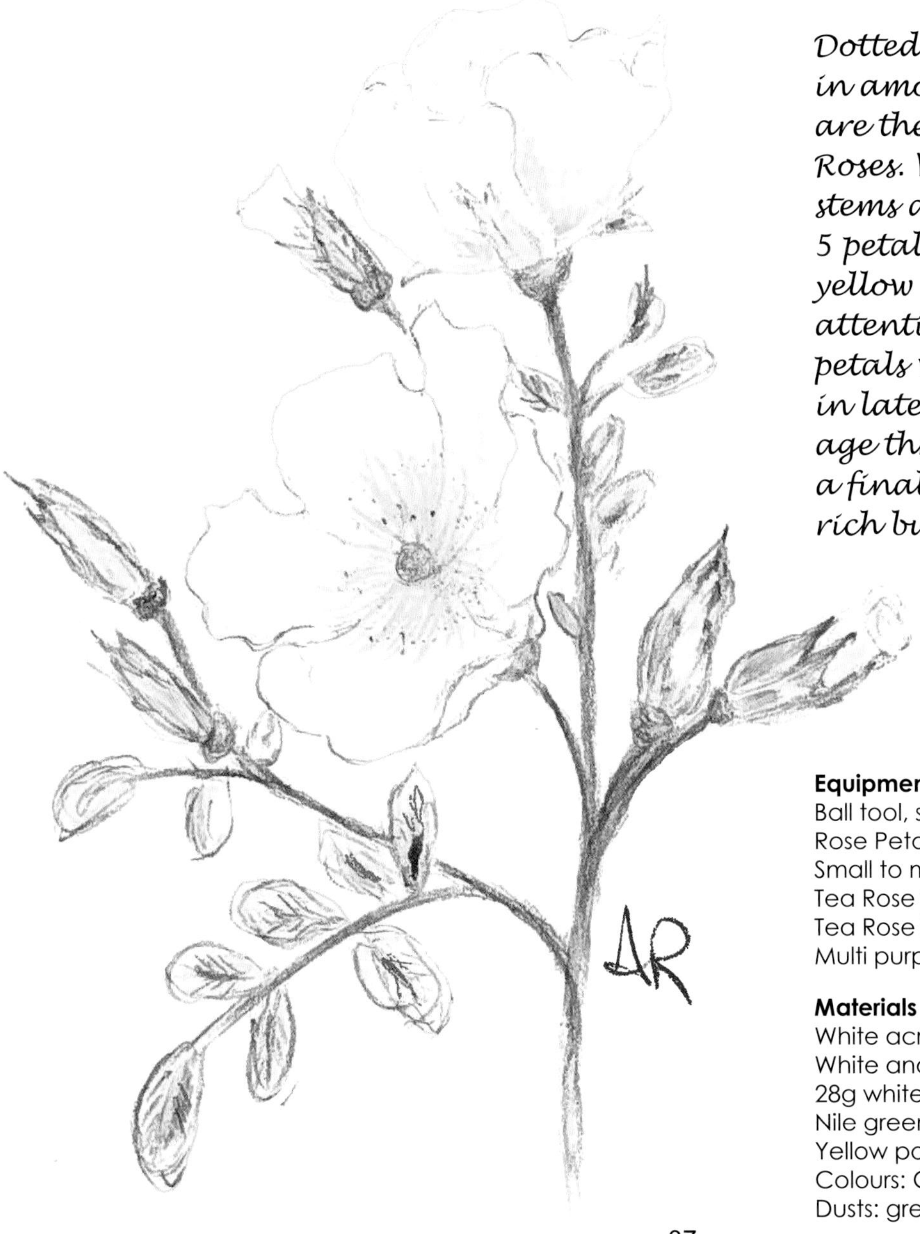

Dotted around the Marsh in amongst the Gorse bushes are these delightful Wild Roses. With their woody stems and small leaves, these 5 petal beauties have bright yellow centres to catch your attention. Clean white petals when they first open in late July they gracefully age through to October with a final flourish of plump rich burgundy hips.

Equipment
Ball tool, scalpel
Rose Petal Cutters KB 0052
Small to medium calyx cutters
Tea Rose petal veiner SKGI
Tea Rose leaf veiner SKGI
Multi purpose metal leaf cutters

Materials
White acrylic paint - cold porcelain
White and pale green paste
28g white & 26, 20g green wire
Nile green florist tape
Yellow pollen
Colours: Gooseberry liquid paste,
Dusts: greens, yellow, red and brown

Buds

1. Roll a slim cone of paste and insert onto a glued hooked 28g wire. Tape the stem with 1/4 width Nile green tape.

2. From white paste cut out 2 petals and soften the edges.

3. Glue the cone, place against the bottom of the petal and wrap the petal completely around the cone leaving it open at the top.

4. Add the 2nd petal over the join of the first petal, wrap around and secure. Dust the base of the petal very lightly with pale yellow.

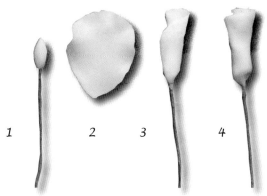

1   2   3   4

5. Cut out a calyx, soften with the ball tool, make small cuts with your scalpel in the sepals. Colour with shades of green and touch the edges with red.

6. Insert the petal bud down through the calyx and secure. Roll a small hip of green paste and secure to the base of the bud. Dust as for the calyx.

Closed Buds

7. Roll a small cone, glue and insert a 28g hooked wire. Cut out a calyx as at point 5, glue and insert the cone down through the centre securing the sepals tightly around the cone. Add a hip and colour as before.

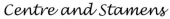

5   6

7

Centre and Stamens

8. Bend a 10cm length of 28g wire in half. Twist a small loop in the top at the bend.

9. Wrap cream thread around two fingers approx 30 times. Twist into a figure of eight. Hook the wire over the middle of the stamens and twist tightly to secure. Cut through the stamens.

10. Roll a small ball of white paste, glue the wire, and stick the ball on top. Pull back the threads, lightly glue the centre and dip into yellow pollen.

11. Lightly dab glue onto the cut stamens and dip into darker yellow pollen. Tape the stem with 1/4 width Nile green tape.

8   9   10   11

Petals

12. From white paste and using a rose petal cutter, cut out 5 petals per flower. Glue and insert a 28g white wire. Tape 2cm down the stem with 1/4 width Nile green tape.

13. Soften the edges and shape the petal into a heart by stretching and spreading up from the bottom to the top sides leaving the centre.

14. Vein with the SKGI Tea Rose veiner. Dust very lightly around the base of the petal with a soft yellow. Cup the petal by gently moulding with your thumb and leave to dry. A cardboard fruit tray works well as a former.

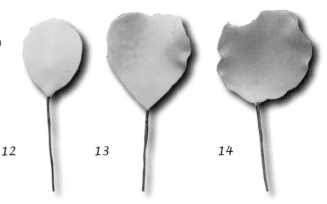

12　　　*13*　　　*14*

15. Bend the wire at the base of the petal and tape tightly to the bottom of the stamens with 1/4 width Nile green tape. Add in the other petals allowing them to overlap eachother so they fit comfortably together.

16. Cut, shape and colour a calyx as for the buds, attach to the base of the flower and then add a little hip to finish off.

16

Leaves

The leaves on this rose are quite small. I use the smallest metal leaf cutter and stretch the paste a to get a few larger ones - just rounding off the tip.

17. Use green paste, 28g wire, soften the edges and vein. Tape the stem 1cm with dark green tape.

18. Dust with darker greens and browns, but use the red to highlight edges. The leaves can also be dark green - the choice is yours! Tape in sets of 3, 5 & 7.

17

18

Tip
Vary the age of flowers by leaving off a petal or two. A stamen by itself gives a really good effect.

Assembly

Tape together a flower, bud and
leaves into a set using 1/2 width dark
green florist tape. Tape onto a 20g
wire to start the main stem. Make
some other small sprays, and add
onto the stem at intervals. Lightly
dust over the Nile green tape of the
roses and buds to blend into the
main stem, which starts to get more
woody as it grows in the bush. If you
like you can use a brown tape as the
stem becomes thicker.

Suggestion ..
Use the same instructions with
larger rose petal cutters, to make
beautiful Rosa Rugosa as pictured
on page 53

Templates

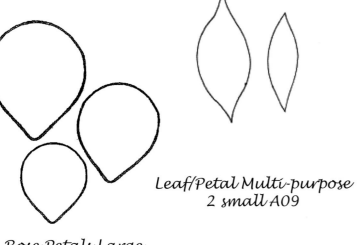

Leaf/Petal Multi-purpose
2 small A09

Rose Petals Large
KB 0052

Calyx A002 (2)

Cold Porcelain Wild Roses

Colouring

Use very pale shades of yellow/green to highlight the veins on the petals, edging some with a nutkin brown. Paint a little terracotta onto the tip of some stamens.

Primrose, Cream, Cyclamen, Nutkin, Spring Green, Leaf Green, Moss green and Terracotta

CLEMATIS - Bill Mackenzie

This beautiful Clematis completely covers one wall of the workshop outside the back door. Strikingly vibrant in colour with a mass of rich yellow flowers complemented by delicate fresh green foliage, it is a cheerful sight from the kitchen window - whatever the weather!

Flowering constantly from late July to October, when the petals fall they are replaced by a 'puffball' of soft stamens which last long into with Winter months.

Equipment
Ball tool, scalpel, scissors
Clematis Petal Cutters TT
Clematis Montana Leaf Cutters TT
Clematis Montana Petal Veiner TT
Peony Leaf Veiner SKGI

Materials
White acrylic paint - cold porcelain
Pale green and pale yellow paste
28, 26, 20g green wire
Nile green, light brown florist tape, yellow pollen
Colours: Gooseberry and melon liquid paste,
Dusts: Yellows, greens and brown

Centre and Stamens

1. Bend an 12cm length of 28g wire in half. Twist a small loop 0.5cm in the top at the bend.

2. Roll a piece of cream paste into a 1.5cm slim oval . Glue the wire, insert into the paste and secure.

3. Glue the oval and sprinkle yellow pollen over to cover completely.

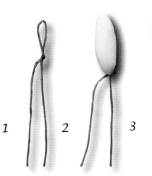

1   2   3

4

4. Spin and twist 4 x 50cm lengths of 1/4 width brown tape. Wrap around 2 fingers, twist into a figure of eight and pinch together in the centre.

5. Hook the wire over the middle of the stamens and twist tightly to secure.

6. Cut through the taped stamens, separate and spread them around the centre. Tape the full stem with 1/4 width Nile green tape.

5   6

7. Roll out some white paste and cut out 4 petals per flower. Soften the edges and vein. Tape with 1/4 width Nile green tape.

8. Bend the tip of the petal backwards. Colour both sides of the petal with a strong bright yellow.

9. Dust lightly down the centre of the outside petal with spring green but highlighting the tip more strongly.

10. Cup the petals and leave them to dry. A cardboard fruit tray is good for this. Make sure the tip of the petal doesn't lose it's bend!

7   8   9

10

43

11. Tape the petals one by one evenly around the centre, tucking them tightly under the base of the stamens.

12. Leave a little space between each petal if you can, but don't worry if they overlap slightly. Tape to the bottom of the stem.

13. Bend the wire about 1cm from the base of the flower allowing the head to hang down.

11 & 12

12

13

Buds

14. Roll a fat cone from cream paste. Glue and insert a hooked 28g wire. Pinch 4 ridges down he side and up to the point. Dust with yellow and spring green.

14

Leaves

15. Use 28g wire and pale green paste for all leaves. With the large cutter, stretch the paste to create length and then snip some more breaks into the leaf.

16. With the medium cutter shorten the length, spread the width with a ball tool and vein.

17. Colour with medium to bright greens, adding a touch of yellow towards the outside.

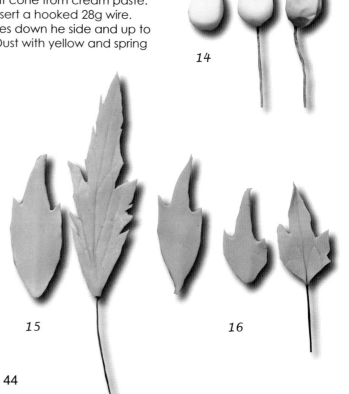

15

16

17

Assembly

This is another typical example of a rambling Clematis. In appearance it is much lighter in weight than other species, however if you try to break off a stem it's as tough as old boot leather! Freedom of expression prevails in assembly so you can attach the flowers, buds and leaves as you wish.

To start I suggest you tape together a flower, bud and set of 2 leaves using 1/2 width Nile green florist tape. Tape onto a 20g wire to give strength. From there add leaves, flowers and buds at varied intervals to the stem.

Spin and twist some 1/4 width Nile green tape and attach to the stem periodically at different lengths to act as tendrils.

Templates

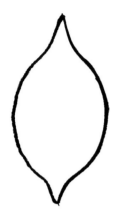

TT Clematis Petal Cutter

TT Clematis Montana Leaves

Cold Porcelain Clematis 'Bill Mackenzie'

Colouring

Use strong yellows to create this stunning flower. Dust darker in the centre of each petal and just touch the edge with brown in places to make older flowers.

Lemon, Egg Yellow, Daffodil, Primrose, Spring Green, Moss Green, Leaf Green, Nutkin Brown

THISTLES & HEATHER

When I was young .... in the summer holidays we used to go and stay with my grandmother in the Borders. Usually a family gathering of uncles, aunties and cousins, we would all head off into the hills and have picnics amongst the purple thistles and the pink heathers. Settling by the Caddon Water, we rolled up our trousers and headed into the river to play with the warm sun on our backs.

Every Summer I am reminded of those happy carefree days as I walk with my lovely dog Beth through the moorland and glens where I live.

Equipment
Ball tool, small nail scissors, cel stick
Thistle leaf cutters Tinker Tech (TT)
Thistle leaf veiner SKGI

Materials
White acrylic paint - cold porcelain
White and green paste
28, 26, 22g 20g green wire
Nile green & dark green florist tape
Purple thread, emery board
Very small seed stamens
Colours: Spruce green liquid paste,
Dusts: Pinks, purples, greens and eucalyptus

THISTLES

Tufts

1. Wrap purple cotton thread around two fingers about 100 times. (The more wraps the bigger the tufts!)

2. Make into a figure of eight, hook over a 22g green wire and twist to secure.

3. Bend up the threads and tape the wire, including the base of the of the threads with 1/2 width green tape. Snip through the threads and fluff up the tips with an emery board.

1   *2*   *3*

4   *5*   *6*

Ball

4. Roll a ball of green paste to suit the size of your tufts.

5. Glue around the neck of the threads Insert down through the centre of the paste and secure.

6. With sharp nail scissors, curve of the blade facing out, hold your thistle upside down make shallow snips into the paste. (Have a practice on a piece of paste to see the many different effects cuts can make.) Dust with greens and eucalyptus.

Leaves

7. From green paste, roll and cut out your leaves, insert a 26g green wire, soften the edges and vein either with a veiner or as I do, use your cel stick to make veins onto the leaf.

8. Keep the points of the leaf sharp and colour with dark and medium green, brushing over the top with some eucalyptus. Tape the stems with 1/4 width green tape.

Assembly

Tape the leaves to the thistle in pairs, starting with the smaller ones at the top.

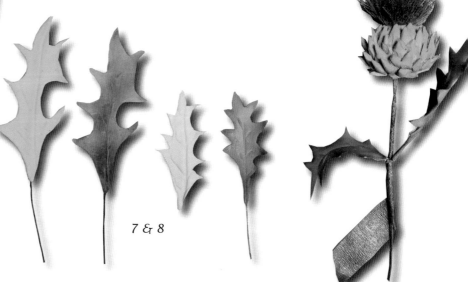

7 & 8

HEATHER

Buds & Flowers

1. Roll a small teardrop of paste, make a hole in the top with a pointed tool and insert a tiny stamen down through the top and secure.

2. Roll a small teardrop, snip around the top edge with sharp scissors and insert a stamen down through the middle and secure.

3. Colour your buds and flowers to suit your arrangement. A mix of plum and violet give a good shade.

1

2

4. Tape the buds onto a 28g wire with 1/4 width Nile green tape. Roll a thin tube of green paste, stick it around the wire and give it a couple of snips.

3

4

5. Roll a thin tube of green paste.

6. Insert a 28g wire and pull the paste down the stem. Use sharp nail scissors to snip very fine cuts into the paste. Vary the colours from light to dark green depending on the look you want.

5

6

Assembly
Tape a group of sprigs of flowers and foliage together using 1/4 width brown or dark green tape.

Thistles and Heather are perfect together - just the two of them. Very popular for a wedding corsage and buttonhole. I love to include them in an arrangement of pink Roses and Ivy where their natural beauty shines and they receive equal attention.

The arrangement below includes Escallonia and Hydrangea Petiolaris both of which can be found as subjects in my 2nd book 'Down the garden Path. Mix and match is the name of the game, never limit yourself. Be inspired and spread your skills from one flower to another.

Cold Porcelain Handel Roses, Thistles, Hydrangea Petiolaris, Escallonia, Thistles and Heather

Templates

Thistle Leaves
TT - Large, Med & small

Colouring

Thistles tufts are strong rich pink or purple, but change the colour to your preference. Catch the spikes of the thistle with a darker green. For the Heather use a blend of pinks and purples - you can't go wrong.

Pink, Plum, Lavender, Violet, Spring Green, Moss Green, Leaf Green, Eucalyptus

A stunning vase of Cold Porcelain Summer Flowers including Foxgloves, Rosa Rugosa and Peony from this book, 'Blooming Lovely' arranged together with Pieris, Catkins and Mini Chrysanthemums detailed in my book 'Down the Garden Path'.

Cosmos

Using the techniques set out for making the Clematis Montana petals on p22 and shaping your petals slightly more rounded with the ball tool, make this beautiful cosmos in a range of colours to enjoy.

For the centre, use a Daisy centre mould, and with surgical tweezers pinch thin strips around the outside edge. Make these slightly raised above the centre. Dust the centre with yellow and dab a little glue onto the tips of the raised pinches. Dip these into strong yellow pollen - et voilà! - instant stamens.

Rosa Rugosa

This variety of Rosa Rugosa is abundant along the hedgerows. With flowers ranging from 6 - 9 cm dia, they are striking in colour from white, through pink to deep fuchsia/magenta. Using the techniques for the Wild Roses on p37 just increase the size of the petals, the stamen centre and calyx to match. Remember to use wires to suit the weight of the new petals.

There are normally at least 7 or 9 leaves per stem - all very similar in size and these are a vibrant green in colour.

Paeonia tenufolia - Sarah Bernhardt

This Peony is definitely worth the effort and creates a very impressive WOW! factor. Base the 3 seed pods around the techniques for the Helleborus Orientalis detailed on page 73 in Down the Garden Path, just make them a little fatter and don't allow the wire to come through the top.

The petals have been made using the KIT BOX Horse Chestnut Leaf shown in my book Autumn Glory. Gently squash the cutter narrower and cut out lots of fine petals of all sizes. Use 30/28g wire and dust the bottom half of the petal for maximum impact.

CHRISTMAS FLOWERS

Christmas is a time of year that I start to look forward to as soon as the clocks go back in October! As the garden begins to hibernate, I feel relieved that I am no longer at battle with the weeds and therefore have a little more time to concentrate on something special for the festive season!

Shades of White, Red and Green are truly symbolic with this time of year and with careful use of these colours it is possible to make strong and bold statements or softer, warmer floral arrangements to showcase your skills and decorate your home.

To make the wired arrangement pictured, I used single Poinsettia bracts taped together in threes and placed to complement large white Snowball Roses. Add in a couple of sprigs of Bittersweet to give length along with the dark green Ivy plus berries creating depth, finished off with a contemporary version of Snowberries and the traditional sprig of Holly this all combines to give a classic yet modern twist on traditional flowers. Add a few Swarovski' Crystals on silver wire to add sparkle as they catch the candle flame.

POINSETTIA

A beautiful and vibrant plant to brighten the darkest of Winter days. When is appears in the shops the Poinsettia with its voluptuous striking red blooms brings a tingle of excitement for the festivities ahead. A fairly hardy plant if it is kept away from drafts. As long as the flower remains in bloom, mince pies and mulled wine remain on the menu at The Yews! - What an excuse :-)

Equipment
Ball tool, scalpel, small sharp scissors
Poinsettia Cutters FMM
Poinsettia Veiner SKGI

Materials
White acrylic paint - cold porcelain
Red, pale green & cream paste
30, 28, 26 green wire
Red and yellow florist tape
Gooseberry green & red extra liquid paste.
Colours: Poinsettia, reds & aubergine, greens and yellows

Centre Buds

1. Roll a small ball of pale green paste, insert a hooked 30g wire 6cm long and gently pull the paste down the wire about 1cm into a upside down teardrop.

2. Snip around the top and centre of the bud with sharp scissors. Your aim is to rough up the top without changing the shape. Make 9 in total for one flower.

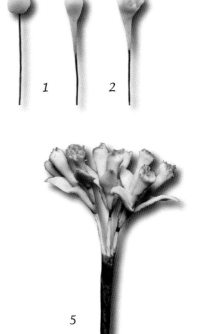

3. Dust the bud with light green and yellow, and brush red over the roughed up top so the colour catches the snips.

4. Roll a 1cm thin cone of cream paste. Pinch flat between your fingers and secure the base of the tiny bract to the bottom of the bud. Dust with light green and yellow. Tape three buds together using yellow florist tape. No need to individually tape the stems of the buds.

5. Tape three sets of 3 buds together. Don't be afraid to push them closely together as a bunch as this will be making a very effective centre for the flower.

Centre Bracts

6. Roll three thin cones 2cm in length from cream paste. Insert a 28g wire 6cm long. Press flat between your finger and thumb, soften the edges and vein with the Poinsettia veiner. Colour with a hint of green and lightly brush red up through the centre vein. Tape the stem 2cm down with 1/4 width red florist tape.

7. Tape the 3 centre bracts equally placed around the buds with red florist tape. At this time add in a 22g wire, 15cm in length to help give strength for when you add on the main red and green bracts.

Tip
You can use one of the small bract cutters for this if you like, but I find it just as easy to use my fingers!

Bracts

There is no exact number of bracts to a flowers, each one is as individual as we are. For the red bracts, I suggest you cut out 5 of each of the 3 larger sizes and 3 of each of the smaller bracts. The template shows 5 sizes only.

9. Colour up some vibrant red paste. Cut our your bracts, insert a 28g wire 6cm long, soften the edges and vein. Try not to lose the points. If you do, use you hands to pinch them back in.

10. Dust the bracts with rich reds, using a darker aubergine at the base and centre. Apply a little bright green to the tips.

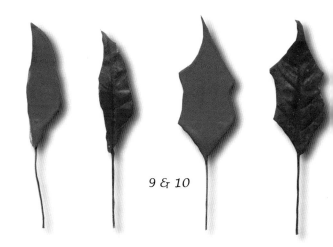

9 & 10

11

11. From pale green paste, cut out 7 large bracts. Dust with strong bright greens, lighter towards the edges adding a hint of red down through the centre and around the edges. Tape all stems with red florist tape.

12

Assembly

12. Tape the smallest red bracts to the base of the central buds leaving a 2-3mm stem on each bract. This allows the bracts to move and fit well against eachother.

Tip
If you do not have coloured tapes, use white tape and brush over with appropriate colour of dusting powder for desired effect.

13. Continue around the flower increasing the size of the bracts as you go. Do not be afraid to mix sizes to fill in gaps. Try not to travel too far down the stem as you tape with the first layers to avoid a long and lanky flower!

14. As you tape the larger red and green bracts onto the main stem, leave a slightly longer stem on each bract to extend their individual length and therefore create a larger flower.

13

14

Templates

Poinsettia cutters FMM

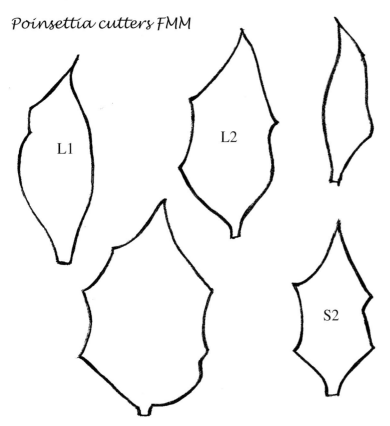

A single Cold Porcelain Poinsettia hooked around a napkin, will make a stunning Christmas table decoration!

Colouring

The colour palette below is only a guide. The Poinsettia is a striking flowers so use bright reds to really bring the flower head to life shading with the darker ones. Don't be afraid to mix your colours, it's fantastic how many variations of shade you can achieve, each adding a richness to any flower :-)

Cyclamen, Aubergine, Poinsettia, Red, Spring Green, Leaf Green, Moss Green and Daffodil

MISTLETOE AND HOLLY

Along with Mulled Wine and Mince Pies, Mistletoe and Holly are most probably among the first things that people connect straight away with the anticipation of Christmas approaching. Quick and easy to make, these berries can be used to decorate anything from wreaths to cards, presents and table settings galore .You just cant go wrong!

With huge embarrassment I remember at one Christmas school dance, standing not quite under the Mistletoe, but pretty darn close to it, hoping that Gordon Nesbit would walk by and plant a kiss on my cheek!

Equipment
Ball tool, scalpel
Holly Leaf Cutters
Holly Leaf Veiner

Materials
White, pale green and red paste
30, 28, 24g green wire
Nile green florist tape
Colours: Gooseberry Green & Red paste,
Dusts: spring, medium & dark green, red, yellow

Mistletoe

Berries

1. Roll a small ball of white paste. If using cold porcelain do not put in acrylic paint to start with. This will allow the paste to dry with a wax look - just like the real berries.

2. Glue and insert a 30g. Push the wire through he ball until you fee it against your finger at the top.

3. Dust the base of the ball with a touch of moss green.

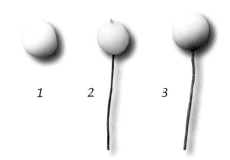

1   2   3

Leaves

4. Roll a slim cone of green paste. Glue and insert a 28g wire into the thick end.

5. Press flat between your first finger and thumb. Gently shape the leaf by curving it towards the top.

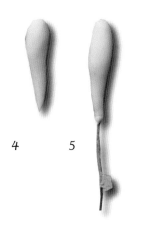

4   5

6 & 7

6. Vein with a cel stick or cocktail stick by marking straight lines from top to bottom.

7. Dust with mid to light greens. Make a few leave ranging from 1.5 - 5cm in length.

8. Tape over the top of a 24g wire, add in two leaves. Tape onto a bunch of berries and continue adding leaves and berries to suit.

Varnish with a matt spray, or if using cold porcelain - hairspray!

8

Holly

Berries

1. Roll a small ball of strong red paste. If using cold porcelain put in acrylic paint to start with before you add the red.

2. Glue and insert a 30g green wire. Do not let the wire come through the top.

3. In some of the berries make a small indent into the top and leave others just round balls. Allow to dry and dip into full strength confectioners varnish to get a really bright shine.

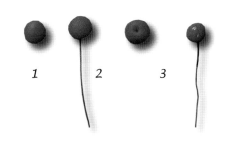

Leaves

4. Roll out some green paste leaving it slightly thicker at one end. Place the cutter over the paste with the bottom at the thicker end and cut out.

5. Insert a 28g wire into the thicker end of the paste, soften around the edges with a ball tool and vein either by hand or with a veiner.

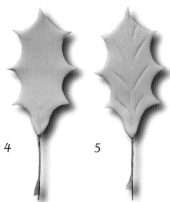

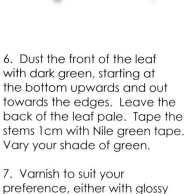

6. Dust the front of the leaf with dark green, starting at the bottom upwards and out towards the edges. Leave the back of the leaf pale. Tape the stems 1cm with Nile green tape. Vary your shade of green.

7. Varnish to suit your preference, either with glossy confectioners varnish or give the leaves a matt finish.

8. Tape leaves and berries onto a 24g wire with Nile or dark green tape adding in berries in groups along the way.

Assembly

Tape together couple of sprigs of Holly and a sprig of Mistletoe. You could add a ribbon at the base and hang just above the front door to catch out any unsuspecting visitors!

Templates

Mistletoe - hand drawn

Holly leaves - hand drawn

Colouring

Be adventurous with your colouring. Use the colour shades below to make the 'Princess Diana' Alstromeria, but experiment with pinks, oranges, reds - there are so many variations to choose from. If you don't have a garden centre nearby, just Google Alstromeria images and take your pick!

Primrose, Daffodil, Burgundy, Red, Spring Green, Leaf Green, Forrest Green and Brown

Table Decorations

This neat spray of Poinsettia, Holly, Mistletoe, White Heather and Ivy works really well fixed to the base of a candle stick or on the side of a wreath.

Using the Poinsettia as the central flower, tape the stems of the other sprays all into the same point. Position each stem at a different length to create the desired shape. Do not travel down the main stem whilst taping as this will leave gaps and your spray will become lanky! You want to keep it nice and tight.

Three of these sprays evenly spaced around a wreath, with some red and gold ribbon is extremely effective and striking as a decoration hanging in a hallway. Alternatively, lie the wreath flat with a big Church Candle in the centre for an equally impressive display.

Substitute the Poinsettia with a large white or red rose, with some warm orange rose buds, rose leaves plus some Fir Cones to change the mood. The wonderful thing about Cold Porcelain Flowers is that you can take them apart and re-use them in different arrangement as many times as you like!

Below are suggestions for some other subjects to make based on the techniques shown.

Symphoricarpos *(Snowberries)*

Roll a mix of bead shape white balls in varied sizes, and insert 30g wire. Use fingers to squash the side to change shape, make an indent in the top and pinch up with tweezers to mark. Colour as shown and tape into tight groups.

Cowberries

Use paste without acrylic added. Roll some balls, insert a 30g wire and snip a little calyx into the bottom of the ball with scissors. Use a cel stick to indent the top. Tear a little paste from he side of some to look nibbled! Paint with mix of reds, brown and white as below.

Quick Fir Cones

Using the same technique as for the thistles, roll a cone of brown paste and snip into the side. Dust with Nutkin and Brown with a touch of green. Use dark brown/black tape to attach and make a small branch stem.

A little note from me ...

After an extremely frustrating day when it seemed nothing was going right, my father once said to me ...

"Aly, have patience with yourself as it is a strength that will build foundations and in time produce results".

I try to apply these words of wisdom to many aspects of my life to varying degrees of success, but in particular when making my flowers. Sometimes my enthusiasm takes over and I find myself at the end wishing I was still in the middle taking a little more time!

I hope you enjoy the collection within..

Best wishes

Alyson R

Suppliers

KIT BOX
Metal stainless steel cutters
Unit 3 Neads Court
Knowles Road
Clevedon
Somerset BS21 7XS
www.kitbox.co.uk
support@kitbox.info
01275 879030 tel/fax

FMM Sugarcraft
Plastic Cutters
Unit 7 Chancerygate Business Park
Whiteleaf Road
Hemel Hempstead
Herts
HP3 9HD
www.fmmsugarcraft.com
sales@fmmsugarcraft.com
01442 292970 tel

Squires Kitchen
Great Impressions veiner
The Grange
Hones Yard
Farnham
Surrey GU9 8BB
www.squires-shop.com
customer@squires-shop.com
0845 6171810 tel

Tårtdecor Sweden AB
Everything you need
www.tartdecor.se
Utmarksvägen 18
442 39 KUNGÄLV
+46 0303 51470 tel
+46 0303 243099 fax

Acknowledgement

Once again my thanks to Colin Brown and his team at MMS Almac Ltd, for their continued unwavering support. Colin, you may have a little less hair and a few more wrinkles but your patience and critical eye coupled with the fact that you haven't yet left the country is very much appreciated! Thank you :-)

If you would like to learn more about cold porcelain, arrange a demonstration or attend a workshop, please do not hesitate to contact me at
alyson@alyson-reynolds.co.uk
or visit the website on
www.alyson-reynolds.co.uk